CW00468177

WeightWatcher
COOKBOOK
New Complete

Tasty & Healthy

Freestyle Program

By: Aida Bugg

Table Of Content

Chapter 1: Breakfast and Brunch

Chapter 2: Chicken And Poultry

Chapter 3: Soups And Stews

Chapter 4: Beef And Pork

Chapter 5: Vegan And Vegetarian

Chapter 6: Fish And Seafood Recipes

Bonus In The End

HIT YOUR WEIGHT

LOSS GOAL

Chapter 1:

Breakfast Recipes

Breakfast

Servings: 4

SmartPoints: 6

Prep + Cooking Time
20 minutes

Nutritional Values (Per Serving):

- Calories: 229
- Fat: 23g
- Carbohydrates: 10g
- Protein: 12g
- Saturated Fat: 4g
- Sodium: 801mg
- Fiber: 2g

Egg And Avocado Toast

Ingredients

- 2 and ½ slices whole wheat bread
- Olive oil spray
- Fresh ground pepper
- Hot sauce to taste
- Salt to taste
- 45g avocado flesh, mashed
- 2 large eggs

Steps to Cook

1. Take your bread slices and make a hole in the middle using a cookie cutter
2. Season avocado mash with salt and pepper
3. Take a skillet and place it over medium-low heat, grease with cooking spray
4. Place bread slices and a cut portion in the skillet
5. Break the egg into the hole of the bread, cook until the egg properly settles down, season with more salt and pepper
6. Flip and cook the other side
7. Once done, transfer to a plate
8. Top the egg with avocado mash, hot sauce and crumble bread (made from the cut piece)
9. Enjoy!

Breakfast

Servings: 4

SmartPoints: 4

Prep + Cooking Time
15 minutes

Egg And Tomato Scramble

Nutritional Values (Per Serving):

- Calories: 130
- Fat: 10g
- Carbohydrates: 8g
- Protein: 1.8g
- Saturated Fat: 3g
- Sodium: 1070mg
- Fiber: 1g

Ingredients

- 8 whole eggs
- 125g fresh basil, chopped
- 30ml olive oil
- 2.5g red pepper flakes, crushed
- 250g grape tomatoes, chopped
- Salt and pepper to taste

Steps to Cook

1. Take a bowl and whisk in eggs, salt, pepper, red pepper flakes and mix well
2. Add tomatoes, basil, and mix
3. Take a skillet and place it over medium-high heat
4. Add egg mixture and cook for 5 minutes and cooked and scrambled
5. Enjoy!

Breakfast

Servings: 7-8

SmartPoints: 4

Prep + Cooking Time
40 minutes

Oats Apple Breakfast Cake

Nutritional Values (Per Serving):

- Calories - 164
- Fat – 4.5g
- Carbohydrates – 32g
- Fiber – 4g
- Sodium – 104mg
- Protein – 3g

Ingredients

- 250g oats
- 500g flour, whole wheat or all-purpose
- 125g stevia granular or raw honey
- 1g salt
- 500g diced apples
- 125ml applesauce
- 125ml almond milk
- 5ml vanilla extract
- 1g baking soda
- 10g cinnamon

Steps to Cook

1. In a mixing bowl (heat-proof), mix all the mentioned ingredients.
2. Take an Instant Pot; open the top lid.
3. Pour 1 cup water and place steamer basket/trivet inside the cooking pot.
4. Arrange the bowl over the basket/trivet.
5. Close the top lid and make sure the valve is sealed.
6. Press "MANUAL" cooking function. Adjust cooking time to 20-25 minutes.
7. Allow pressure to build and cook the ingredients for the set time.
8. After the set cooking time ends, press "CANCEL" and then press "NPR". Instant Pot will slowly and naturally release the pressure for 8- 10 minutes.
9. Open the top lid, add the cooked mixture in serving plates.
10. Serve warm.

Breakfast

Servings: 5-6

SmartPoints: 4

Prep + Cooking Time
19 minutes

Nutritional Values (Per Serving):

- Calories - 227
- Fat – 14g
- Carbohydrates – 7g
- Fiber – 1g
- Sodium - 374mg
- Protein – 14.5g

Cheese Tomato Omelet

Ingredients

- 60g tomato paste
- 5g salt
- 5 eggs
- 125ml milk
- 15g turmeric
- 125g cilantro, minced
- 15g butter
- 120g Parmesan cheese, shredded

Steps to Cook

1. Whisk the eggs with the milk and tomato paste in the mixing bowl. Mix in the salt and turmeric.
2. Mix in the cheese and cilantro.
3. Take an Instant Pot; open the top lid.
4. Press "SAUTÉ" cooking function.
5. In the cooking pot area, add the butter and melt it.
6. Add in the egg mixture and spread it to make a round shape.
7. Close the top lid and make sure the valve is sealed.
8. Press "STEAM" cooking function. Adjust cooking time to 8 minutes.
9. Allow pressure to build and cook the ingredients for the set time.
10. After the set cooking time ends, press "CANCEL" and then press "QPR". Instant Pot will quickly release pressure.
11. Open the top lid, add the cooked mixture in serving plates.
12. Serve warm.

Breakfast

Servings: 4-6

SmartPoints: 2

Prep + Cooking Time
20 minutes

Ham Egg Frittata

Nutritional Values (Per Serving):

- Calories - 215
- Fat – 13g
- Carbohydrates – 6.5g
- Fiber – 1g
- Sodium - 346mg
- Protein – 17.5g

Ingredients

- 220g ham, chopped
- 5g white pepper
- 15g lemon zest
- 5ml olive oil
- 5g salt
- 2.5g paprika
- 125g parsley, chopped
- 7 eggs
- 125ml milk
- 1 tomato, chopped

Steps to Cook

1. Beat the eggs in the mixing bowl. Mix in the milk, salt, paprika, white pepper, and lemon zest.
2. Blend the mix in a blender. Mix in the ham and tomatoes.
3. Take an Instant Pot; open the top lid.
4. Coat the pot using cooking oil. Add the ham mix in the cooking pot. Top with the parsley.
5. Close the top lid and make sure the valve is sealed.
6. Press "STEAM" cooking function. Adjust cooking time to 10 minutes.
7. Allow pressure to build and cook the ingredients for the set time.
8. After the set cooking time ends, press "CANCEL" and then press "QPR". Instant Pot will quickly release pressure.
9. Open the top lid, add the cooked mixture in serving plates.
10. Serve warm.

Breakfast

Servings: 2

Freestyle Points per Serving: 1

Prep + Cooking Time
15 minutes

Nutritional Values (Per Serving):

- Calories – 237
- Fat – 1g
- Saturated Fats – 0g
- Trans Fats - 0g
- Carbohydrates – 23g
- Fiber – 6g
- Sodium – 396mg
- Protein – 9g

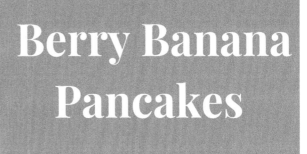

Berry Banana Pancakes

Ingredients

- 5g baking powder
- 1 banana, mashed well
- 1g cinnamon
- 5g vanilla
- 2 egg whites

Steps to Cook

1. Take a skillet or saucepan (medium size preferable); heat it over medium cooking flame.
2. Take a mixing bowl (either medium or large size), crack and whisk the egg whites.
3. Stir in the cinnamon, vanilla, and baking powder.
4. Add the banana and mix; divide batter into 4 parts.
5. Add the batter, spread to make round and cook for 2 minutes, flip and cook for 30-45 seconds more.
6. Repeat process for remaining batter. Serve with fresh berries.

Breakfast

Servings: 4   **Freestyle Points per Serving: 4**   **Prep + Cooking Time**
55 minutes

Breakfast Casserole

Nutritional Values (Per Serving):

- Calories – 376
- Fat – 9g
- Saturated Fats – 3g
- Trans Fats - 0g
- Carbohydrates – 36g
- Fiber – 12g
- Sodium – 752mg
- Protein – 24g

Ingredients

- 4 eggs
- 10g cinnamon
- 250ml milk
- 330g egg whites
- 2 apples, peeled and cut to dice
- 8 slices bread, low calorie

Steps to Cook

1. Lightly grease a casserole dish (9x13-inch) with cooking spray. Preheat an oven to 350°F.
2. In a microwave-safe mixing bowl, mix 1 teaspoon cinnamon and apples.
3. Microwave the mix for 2-3 minutes.
4. In the dish, add the bread slices and cooked apples.
5. In a mixing bowl, whisk fresh milk, egg whites, and eggs.
6. Add the mix over the dish; bake for 45 minutes.
7. Serve warm.

Breakfast

Servings: 4

SmartPoints: 1

Prep + Cooking Time
25 minutes

Nutritional Values (Per Serving):

- Calories - 176
- Fat – 2.5g
- Carbohydrates – 34g
- Fiber – 7g
- Sodium - 144mg
- Protein – 13g

Bacon Brussels Sprouts

Ingredients

- 4 bacon slices, center cut, make small pieces
- 3 shallots, finely diced
- 3 garlic cloves, minced
- 450g Brussels sprouts, make halves
- 125ml water

Steps to Cook

1. Take an Instant Pot; open the top lid.
2. Press "SAUTÉ" cooking function.
3. Coat the pot with some olive oil. In the cooking pot area, add the bacon. Cook until turn crisp for 5-6 minutes.
4. Add in the remaining ingredients; combine well.
5. Close the top lid and make sure the valve is sealed.
6. Press "MANUAL" cooking function. Adjust cooking time to 3-5 minutes.
7. Allow pressure to build and cook the ingredients for the set time.
8. After the set cooking time ends, press "CANCEL" and then press "QPR". Instant Pot will quickly release pressure.
9. Open the top lid, add the cooked mixture in serving plates.
10. Serve warm.

Breakfast

Servings: 2

SmartPoints: 6

Prep + Cooking Time
20 minutes

Pumpkin Pie Oatmeal

Nutritional Values (Per Serving):

- Calories: 264
- Fat: 4g
- Carbohydrates: 34g
- Protein: 7g
- Saturated Fat: 1g
- Sodium: 246mg
- Fiber: 4g

Ingredients

- 125g canned pumpkin
- Mashed banana as needed
- 180ml unsweetened almond milk
- 2.5g pumpkin pie spice
- 250g oats
- 10g maple syrup

Steps to Cook

1. Mash banana using fork and mix in the remaining ingredients (except oats) and mix well
2. Add oats and finely stir
3. Transfer mixture to a pot and let the oats cook until it has absorbed the liquid and are tender
4. Serve and enjoy!

Breakfast

Servings: 4

SmartPoints: 5

Prep + Cooking Time
15 minutes

Nutritional Values (Per Serving):

- Calories: 270
- Fat: 4g
- Carbohydrates: 55g
- Protein: 11g
- Saturated Fat: 1g
- Sodium: 129mg
- Fiber: 3g

Hearty Egg Salad

Ingredients

- 1g pepper
- 3g salt
- 1-piece dill
- 30g mayonnaise
- 2.5g Dijon mustard
- 30g chives
- 4 whole eggs
- 2 hardboiled eggs

Steps to Cook

1. Take a pan and fill it with water, add eggs and place on high heat
2. Bring to a boil
3. Once eggs are done, drain water and add eggs to ice water bath
4. Once cooled, remove shells
5. Gently remove yolks from two eggs and slice them up
6. Add pepper, salt, mustard, dill, chives, and mayo to a bowl and stir well, add sliced up egg whites and egg yolks
7. Mix well
8. Enjoy!

Breakfast

Servings: 3

SmartPoints: 2

Prep + Cooking Time
35 minutes

Nutritional Values (Per Serving):

- Calories: 259
- Fat: 3g
- Carbohydrates: 7g
- Protein: 3g
- Saturated Fat: 1g
- Sodium: 216mg
- Fiber: 2g

Banana Custard

Ingredients

- 2 ripe bananas, peeled and mashed finely
- 3ml of vanilla extract
- 400ml unsweetened almond milk
- 3 eggs

Steps to Cook

1. Preheat your oven to 350 degrees Fahrenheit
2. Grease 8 custard glasses lightly
3. Arrange the glasses in a large baking dish
4. Take a large bowl and mix all of the ingredients and mix them well until combined nicely
5. Divide the mixture evenly between the glasses
6. Pour water in the baking dish
7. Bake for 25 minutes
8. Take it out and serve
9. Enjoy!

Chapter 2:

Chicken And Poultry

Servings: 4

SmartPoints: 2

Prep + Cooking Time
22 minutes

Nutritional Values (Per Serving):

- Calories: 330
- Fat: 11g
- Carbohydrates: 20g
- Protein: 23g
- Saturated Fat: 3g
- Sodium: 1005mg
- Fiber: 1g

Delicious Chicken Fried Rice

Ingredients

- 5ml olive oil
- 4 large egg whites
- 1 onion, chopped
- 2 garlic cloves, minced
- 240g skinless chicken breasts, boneless, cut into 1 cm cubes
- 125g carrots, chopped
- 125g of frozen green peas
- 500g long-grain brown rice, cooked
- 45ml soy sauce, low sodium

Steps to Cook

1. Coat skillet with oil, place it over medium-high heat
2. Add egg whites and cook until scrambled
3. Sauté onion, garlic and chicken breasts for 6 minutes
4. Add carrots, peas and keep cooking for 3 minutes
5. Stir in rice, season with soy sauce
6. Add cooked egg whites, stir for 3 minutes
7. Enjoy!

Servings: 5-6

SmartPoints: 5

Prep + Cooking Time
30 minutes

Nutritional Values (Per Serving):

- Calories – 276
- Fat – 2.5g
- Carbohydrates – 12g
- Fiber – 1g
- Sodium - 358mg
- Protein – 23.5g

Potato Chicken Roast

Ingredients

- 2 cloves garlic, minced
- 10g fresh thyme
- 5g black pepper
- 1 large roasting chicken
- 10ml extra-virgin olive oil
- 5g paprika
- 250g baby carrots
- 380ml water
- 5g sea salt
- 2 stalks celery, chopped
- 2 medium potatoes, cubed

Steps to Cook

1. Coat the chicken with the olive oil, garlic, thyme, black pepper, paprika, and salt. Add the celery and carrots inside the chicken cavity.
2. Take an Instant Pot; open the top lid.
3. Add the chicken and water in the cooking pot. Add the potatoes.
4. Close the top lid and make sure the valve is sealed.
5. Press "MANUAL" cooking function. Adjust cooking time to 20 minutes.
6. Allow pressure to build and cook the ingredients for the set time.
7. After the set cooking time ends, press "CANCEL" and then press "NPR". Instant Pot will slowly and naturally release the pressure for 8- 10 minutes.
8. Open the top lid, add the cooked mixture in serving plates. Cook on sauté for a few minutes, if you want to thicken the sauce.
9. Serve warm.

Servings: 5-6

SmartPoints: 7

Prep + Cooking Time
20 minutes

Coconut Curry Chicken

Nutritional Values (Per Serving):

- Calories – 133
- Fat – 11g
- Carbohydrates – 8g
- Fiber – 1.5g
- Sodium - 295mg
- Protein – 6.5g

Ingredients

- 15g curry powder
- 5g turmeric
- 60ml lemon juice
- 1 can full-fat coconut milk
- 3g lemon zest
- 3g salt
- 1.8kg chicken breast, skin removed

Steps to Cook

1. In a mixing bowl, mix the lemon juice, coconut milk, curry powder, turmeric, lemon zest, and salt.
2. Take an Instant Pot; open the top lid.
3. Add the chicken and bowl mix in the cooking pot. Using a spatula, gently stir to combine well.
4. Close the top lid and make sure the valve is sealed.
5. Press "POULTRY" cooking function with default cooking time.
6. Allow pressure to build and cook the ingredients for the set time.
7. After the set cooking time ends, press "CANCEL" and then press "NPR". Instant Pot will slowly and naturally release the pressure for 8- 10 minutes.
8. Open the top lid, add the cooked mixture in serving plates.
9. Serve warm.

Chicken And Poultry

Servings: 5-6

SmartPoints: 0

Prep + Cooking Time
35 minutes

Garlic Salsa Chicken

Nutritional Values (Per Serving):

- Calories – 153
- Fat – 2.5g
- Carbohydrates – 6g
- Fiber – 2g
- Sodium - 421mg
- Protein – 26g

Ingredients

- 1g oregano
- Salt as needed
- 1g garlic powder
- 680g skinless chicken tenders
- 1g ground cumin
- 460g roasted salsa verde

Steps to Cook

1. Mix the oregano, garlic powder, salt, and cumin in a mixing bowl.
2. Coat the chicken with the prepared mix and set aside for 30 minutes to season.
3. Take an Instant Pot; open the top lid.
4. Add the seasoned chicken and salsa in the cooking pot. Using a spatula, gently stir to combine well.
5. Close the top lid and make sure the valve is sealed.
6. Press "MANUAL" cooking function. Adjust cooking time to 18-20 minutes.
7. Allow pressure to build and cook the ingredients for the set time.
8. After the set cooking time ends, press "CANCEL" and then press "QPR". Instant Pot will quickly release pressure.
9. Open the top lid, shred the chicken; add the cooked mixture in serving plates.
10. Serve warm.

Servings: 3-4

SmartPoints: 0

Prep + Cooking Time
25 minutes

Chicken Yogurt Salsa

Nutritional Values (Per Serving):

- Calories - 314
- Fat – 6.5g
- Carbohydrates – 31g
- Fiber – 3.5g
- Sodium - 742mg
- Protein – 31g

Ingredients

- 125ml water or chicken broth
- 4 chicken breasts
- 1 jar salsa
- 250g plain, fat-free Greek yogurt

Steps to Cook

1. Take an Instant Pot; open the top lid.
2. Add all the ingredients in the cooking pot. Using a spatula, gently stir to combine well.
3. Close the top lid and make sure the valve is sealed.
4. Press "MANUAL" cooking function. Adjust cooking time to 15 minutes.
5. Allow pressure to build and cook the ingredients for the set time.
6. After the set cooking time ends, press "CANCEL" and then press "NPR". Instant Pot will slowly and naturally release the pressure for 8- 10 minutes.
7. Open the top lid, add the cooked mixture in serving plates.
8. Serve warm.

Servings: 6

Freestyle Points per Serving: 5

Prep + Cooking Time
40 minutes

Nutritional Values (Per Serving):

- Calories – 263
- Fat – 17g
- Saturated Fats – 9g
- Trans Fats - 0g
- Carbohydrates – 18g
- Fiber – 1g
- Sodium – 742mg
- Protein – 11g

Cheese Cream Chicken

Ingredients

- 1 (220g) package biscuits
- 80g light sour cream
- 60g ranch dressing
- 120g light cream cheese
- 500g cooked shredded chicken
- 5 slices bacon, cooked and crumbled
- 125g low-fat cheese, shredded

Steps to Cook

1. Preheat an oven to 190°C. Grease a baking pan (9x13) with a cooking spray.

2. Crush the biscuits; arrange over the baking pan.

3. Take a mixing bowl (either medium or large size), add in the cream cheese, sour cream, ranch dressing and chicken in the bowl to mix well with each other.

4. Add the mix over the biscuits and spread evenly.

5. Bake for 30 minutes. Serve warm.

Servings: 6

 **Freestyle Points per Serving: 2**

 **Prep + Cooking Time**
25 minutes

Nutritional Values (Per Serving):

- Calories – 142
- Fat – 3g
- Saturated Fats – 1g
- Trans Fats - 0g
- Carbohydrates – 21g
- Fiber – 2g
- Sodium – 642mg
- Protein – 23g

Chicken Veggie Rice

Ingredients

- 1 onion, chopped
- 2 cloves of garlic, minced
- 5ml olive oil
- 4 large egg whites
- 340g skinless chicken breasts make ½" cubes
- 500g long-grain brown rice, cooked
- 45ml soy sauce, low-sodium
- 125g carrots, chopped
- 125g frozen green peas

Steps to Cook

1. Take a skillet or saucepan (medium size preferable); heat it over a medium cooking flame.
2. Add the oil and heat it.
3. Add the egg whites and cook until scrambled. Set it aside.
4. Add and cook the onions, garlic, and chicken breasts for 5-6 minutes until lightly brown. Add the carrots and peas.
5. Cook for 2-3 more minutes.
6. Stir in the rice and soy sauce. Add the cooked egg mix and stir-cook for 2-3 more minutes.
7. Serve warm.

Chicken And Poultry

Servings: 4

SmartPoints: 3

Prep + Cooking Time
25 minutes

Nutritional Values (Per Serving):

- Calories: 300
- Fat: 10g
- Carbohydrates: 10g
- Protein: 43g
- Saturated Fat: 3g
- Sodium: 945mg
- Fiber: 2g

Lemon And Pepper Chicken

Ingredients

- 10ml olive oil
- 560g skinless chicken cutlets
- 2 whole eggs
- 60g panko/BREAD CRUMBS
- 15g lemon pepper
- Salt and pepper to taste
- 750g green beans
- 60g parmesan cheese
- 1g garlic powder

Steps to Cook

1. Preheat your oven to 210 degrees C
2. Take a bowl and stir in seasoning, parmesan, lemon pepper, garlic powder, panko
3. Whisk eggs in another bowl
4. Coat cutlets in eggs and press into panko mix
5. Transfer coated chicken to a parchment-lined a baking sheet
6. Toss the beans in oil, pepper, and salt, lay them on the side of the baking sheet
7. Bake for 15 minutes
8. Enjoy!

Chicken And Poultry

Servings: 4

SmartPoints: 4

Prep + Cooking Time
50 minutes

Nutritional Values (Per Serving):

- Calories: 270
- Fat: 2g
- Carbohydrates: 25g
- Protein: 33g
- Saturated Fat: 0.5g
- Sodium: 450mg
- Fiber: 2g

Grilled BBQ Chicken

Ingredients

- 5g sriracha
- 5g ginger, minced
- 60ml pineapple juice
- 30ml soy sauce
- The 125ml BBQ sauce
- 5g garlic, minced
- 500g pineapple, sliced

Steps to Cook

1. Take a bowl and stir in garlic, sriracha, soy sauce, garlic, BBQ, pineapple juice and mix well
2. Add chicken and let it marinate for 30 minutes
3. Grill pineapple slices and chicken in a hot pan, cook until the internal temperature reaches 165 degrees F and the pineapple are finely caramelized
4. Bring leftover marinade to boil and serve pineapple with chicken and extra sauce
5. Enjoy!

Chicken And Poultry

Servings: 4

SmartPoints: 3

Prep + Cooking Time
45 minutes

Nutritional Values (Per Serving):

- Calories: 540
- Fat: 35g
- Carbohydrates: 25g
- Protein: 33g
- Saturated Fat: 7g
- Sodium: 940mg
- Fiber: 5g

Balsamic Chicken Dish

Ingredients

- 3 boneless chicken breasts, skinless
- Salt and pepper as needed
- 60g of all-purpose flour
- 160ml of low-fat chicken broth
- 7g of corn starch
- 125g of low sugar raspberry preserve
- 22ml of balsamic vinegar

Steps to Cook

1. Cut the chicken breast into bite-sized portions and season with salt and pepper
2. Dredge the meat in flour and shake off any excess
3. Take a non-stick skillet and place it over medium heat
4. Add chicken and cook for 15 minutes, making sure to turn once halfway through
5. Remove chicken and transfer to a platter
6. Add cornstarch, broth, raspberry preserve into the same skillet and stir
7. Stir in balsamic vinegar and keep the heat on medium, stir cook for a few minutes
8. Transfer the chicken back to the skillet and cook for 15 minutes more, turning once
9. Serve and enjoy!

Chapter 3:

Soups And Stews

Servings: 3

SmartPoints: 1

Prep + Cooking Time
32 minutes

Lovely Cabbage Soup

Nutritional Values (Per Serving):

- Calories: 22
- Fat: 0g
- Carbohydrates: 5g
- Protein: 1g
- Saturated Fat: 0g
- Sodium: 759mg
- Fiber: 1g

Ingredients

- 750ml non-fat beef stock
- 2 garlic cloves, minced
- 15g of tomato paste
- 500g cabbage, chopped
- ½ a yellow onion
- 125g carrot, chopped
- 125g green beans
- 125g zucchini, chopped
- 3g of basil
- 3g of oregano
- Salt and pepper as needed

Steps to Cook

1. Grease a pot with non-stick cooking spray
2. Place it over medium heat and allow the oil the heat up
3. Add onions, carrots, and garlic and Sauté for 5 minutes
4. Add broth, tomato paste, green beans, cabbage, basil, oregano, salt, and pepper
5. Bring the whole mix to a boil and lower down the heat, simmer for 5-10 minutes until all veggies are tender
6. Add zucchini and simmer for 5 minutes more
7. Sever hot and enjoy!

Soups And Stews

Servings: 3

SmartPoints: 3

Prep + Cooking Time
45 minutes

Nutritional Values (Per Serving):

- Calories: 122
- Fat: 4g
- Carbohydrates: 9g
- Protein: 11g
- Saturated Fat: 1g
- Sodium: 564mg
- Fiber: 2g

Broccoli And Cheese Delight

Ingredients

- 3 can of 400ml (each) chicken broth
- 2 bag (450g each) frozen broccoli
- 1 can of 280g (each) tomatoes and green chili pepper
- 280g Velveeta low-fat cheese

Steps to Cook

1. Take a pot and add broth, frozen broccoli, tomatoes and chili
2. Mix well and place it over medium-high heat
3. Allow the mixture to heat up and reach a boil
4. Lower down the heat to low and simmer for 25 minutes until the veggies are tender
5. Cube Velveeta and drop them into the soup
6. Simmer until the cheese melts
7. Serve and enjoy!

Soups And Stews

Servings: 4

SmartPoints: 2

Prep + Cooking Time
45 minutes

Nutritional Values (Per Serving):

- Calories: 591
- Fat: 33g
- Carbohydrates: 31g
- Protein: 32g
- Saturated Fat: 8g
- Sodium: 1356mg
- Fiber: 2g

Greek Lemon And Chicken Soup

Ingredients

- 500g cooked chicken, chopped
- 2 medium carrots, chopped
- 125g of onion, chopped
- 60ml lemon juice
- 1 clove garlic, minced
- 1 can cream of chicken soup, fat-free and low sodium
- 2 cans of chicken broth, fat-free
- 1g of ground black pepper
- 160g of long-grain rice
- 30g of parsley, snipped

Steps to Cook

1. Add all of the listed ingredients to a pot (except rice and parsley)
2. Season with salt and pepper
3. Bring the mix to a boil over medium-high heat
4. Stir in rice and set heat to medium
5. Simmer for 20 minutes until rice is tender
6. Garnish parsley, and enjoy!

Servings: 4

SmartPoints: 1

Prep + Cooking Time
30 minutes

Healthy Thai Soup

Nutritional Values (Per Serving):

- Calories: 71
- Fat: 1.8g
- Carbohydrates: 5g
- Protein: 10g
- Saturated Fat: 0.5g
- Sodium: 657mg
- Fiber: 1g

Ingredients

- 750ml chicken stocks
- 15g tom yum paste
- ½ garlic clove, chopped
- 3 stalks lemongrass, chopped
- 2 kaffir lime leaves
- 2 skinless and boneless chicken breast, shredded
- 120g mushrooms, sliced
- 15ml fish sauce
- 15ml lime juice
- 5g green chile pepper, chopped
- 1 bunch coriander, chopped
- 1 bunch coriander, chopped
- 1 sprig fresh basil, chopped

Steps to Cook

1. Take a large-sized saucepan and add chicken stock
2. Bring the mix to a boil
3. Stir in tom yum paste, garlic and cook for 2 minutes
4. Stir in lemongrass, kaffir lime leaves and simmer for 5 minutes over low heat
5. Add mushrooms, fish sauce, green chile, lime juice, pepper and keep cooking over medium heat until blended well
6. Remove the heat and serve warm with a garnish of coriander and basil
7. Enjoy!

Chapter 4:

Beef And Pork

Servings: 4

SmartPoints: 4

Prep + Cooking Time
30 minutes

Beef And Spinach Meatballs

Nutritional Values (Per Serving):

- Calories: 200
- Fat: 8g
- Carbohydrates: 5g
- Protein: 29g
- Saturated Fat: 2g
- Sodium: 658mg
- Fiber: 1g

Ingredients

- 125g onion
- 4 garlic cloves
- 1 whole egg
- 1g oregano
- Salt and pepper to taste
- 450g lean ground beef
- 280g spinach

Steps to Cook

1. Preheat your oven to 190 degrees C
2. Take a bowl and mix in the rest of the ingredients, mix using your hands and roll into meatballs
3. Transfer to a sheet tray and bake for 20 minutes
4. Enjoy!

Servings: 4

SmartPoints: 4

Prep + Cooking Time
30 minutes

Peppered Up Beef Tenderloin

Nutritional Values (Per Serving):

- Calories: 183
- Fat: 9g
- Carbohydrates: 1g
- Protein: 24g
- Saturated Fat: 3g
- Sodium: 2134mg
- Fiber: 0.1g

Ingredients

- 10g sage, chopped
- Salt and pepper
- 1.1kg beef tenderloin
- 10g thyme, chopped
- 2 garlic cloves, sliced
- 10g rosemary, chopped
- 20ml olive oil

Steps to Cook

1. Preheat your oven to 210 degrees C
2. Take a small knife and cut incisions on tenderloin, insert one slice of garlic into the incision
3. Rub meat with oil
4. Take a bowl and add salt, sage, thyme, rosemary, pepper and mix well
5. Rub spice mix over tenderloin
6. Put rubbed tenderloin into roasting pan and bake for 10 minutes
7. Lower temperature to 180 degrees C and cook for 20 minutes more until an internal thermometer read 60 degrees C
8. Transfer tenderloin to cutting board and let them sit for 15 minutes, slice into 20 pieces, and enjoy!

Beef And Pork

Servings: 4

Freestyle Points per Serving: 4

Prep + Cooking Time
20 minutes

Nutritional Values (Per Serving):

- Calories – 327
- Fat – 12g
- Saturated Fats – 5g
- Trans Fats - 0g
- Carbohydrates – 22g
- Fiber – 1g
- Sodium – 642mg
- Protein – 27g

Beef Lettuce Burgers

Ingredients

- 3g salt
- 15ml Worcestershire sauce
- 10g garlic, minced
- 1g pepper
- 4 hamburger buns, low calorie
- 450g ground beef
- Shredded as

Steps to Cook

1. Coat a griddle with some olive oil or cooking spray and heat it.
2. Take a mixing bowl (either medium or large size), add in the pepper, salt, Worcestershire sauce, garlic, and beef in the bowl to mix well with each other.
3. Prepare 4 patties from the mix.
4. Place them over the griddle and cook for 4-5 minutes on each side.
5. Take the buns and make burgers with your favorite toppings, lettuce, and serve.

Servings: 4

Freestyle Points per Serving: 5

Prep + Cooking Time
25 minutes

Creamy Pork Chops

Nutritional Values (Per Serving):

- Calories – 134
- Fat – 5g
- Saturated Fats – 2g
- Trans Fats - 0g
- Carbohydrates – 2g
- Fiber – 0g
- Sodium – 447mg
- Protein – 14g

Ingredients

- 4 pork loin chops, center-cut
- 80g non-fat, half-and-half
- 80ml fat-free chicken stock
- 3g salt
- 22g Dijon mustard
- 3g black pepper
- 3g onion powder
- Pinch of dried thyme

Steps to Cook

1. Rub the salt, pepper, and onion powder over the chops.

2. Take a skillet or saucepan (medium size preferable); heat it over a medium cooking flame.

3. Add the oil and heat it.

4. Add the meat and cook, while stirring, until turns evenly brown for 3-4 minute per side.

5. Pour the stock, mustard, and half-and-half.

6. Lower temperature setting; cook for 6-7 more minutes.

7. When the sauce becomes thick, add the thyme. Serve warm.

Servings: 7-8

SmartPoints: 3

Prep + Cooking Time
50 minutes

Chipotle Beef Roast

Nutritional Values (Per Serving):

- Calories - 217
- Fat – 5g
- Carbohydrates – 9g
- Fiber – 1.5g
- Sodium - 724mg
- Protein – 21g

Ingredients

- 15g ground cumin
- 1 lime, juiced
- 1/2 medium onion, chopped
- 5 cloves of garlic, minced
- 60ml chipotles in adobo sauce
- 250ml water
- 1.36kg beef eye round roast, fat trimmed
- 15g ground oregano
- 3g ground cloves
- 12g salt
- Black pepper as per taste
- 5ml oil
- 3 bay leaves

Steps to Cook

1. Add the onion, garlic, cumin, lime juice, chipotles, oregano, and cloves in a blender. Add water and blend until smooth.

2. Season the beef with pepper and salt.

3. Take an Instant Pot; open the top lid.

4. Press "SAUTÉ" cooking function.

5. In the cooking pot area, add the oil and heat it.

6. Add the beef and cook for 5 minutes until it turns brown on all sides. Add the puree and bay leaves.

7. Close the top lid and make sure the valve is sealed.

8. Press "MANUAL" cooking function. Adjust cooking time to 35 minutes.

9. Allow pressure to build and cook the ingredients for the set time.

10. After the set cooking time ends, press "CANCEL" and then press "QPR". Instant Pot will quickly release pressure.

11. Open the top lid, remove the bay leave and shred the meat.

12. Add the cooked mixture in serving plates, adjust seasoning if needed. Serve warm.

Servings: 6-8

SmartPoints: 3

Prep + Cooking Time
35 minutes

Corn Potato Beef

Nutritional Values (Per Serving):

- Calories – 346
- Fat – 7g
- Carbohydrates – 28.5g
- Fiber – 6g
- Sodium - 546mg
- Protein – 21g

Ingredients

- 750ml beef broth
- 5ml olive oil
- Pepper and salt as needed
- 450g lean beef, make cubes
- 1 bay leaf
- 3g dried oregano
- 1 onion, chopped
- 250g carrots, chopped
- 320g tomato sauce
- 2 garlic cloves, minced
- 250g frozen corn, drained
- 250g celery, chopped
- 380g red potatoes, cubed and skin removed

Steps to Cook

1. Take an Instant Pot; open the top lid.
2. Press "SAUTÉ" cooking function.
3. In the cooking pot area, add the oil, garlic, dried oregano, and onions. Cook until turn translucent and softened for 1-2 minutes.
4. add the meat and cook for about 3–4 minutes to evenly brown.
5. Add the celery, carrots, pepper, and salt; stir-cook for more 3–4 minutes.
6. Add in the remaining ingredients; combine well.
7. Close the top lid and make sure the valve is sealed.
8. Press "MANUAL" cooking function. Adjust cooking time to 15-18 minutes.
9. Allow pressure to build and cook the ingredients for the set time.
10. After the set cooking time ends, press "CANCEL" and then press "NPR". Instant Pot will slowly and naturally release the pressure for 8-10 minutes.
11. Open the top lid, add the cooked mixture in serving plates.
12. Serve warm.

Beef And Pork

Servings: 5-6

SmartPoints: 4

Prep + Cooking Time
25 minutes

Nutritional Values (Per Serving):

- Calories - 243
- Fat – 10.5g
- Carbohydrates – 21.5g
- Fiber – 3g
- Sodium - 586mg
- Protein – 15g

Beef Penne Meal

Ingredients

- 2 white onions, sliced
- 250g ground beef
- 45g chives
- 220g penne
- 5ml olive oil
- 5g salt
- 30ml soy sauce
- 5g turmeric
- 1 L chicken stock
- 125g tomato sauce
- 5g cilantro
- 7g paprika

Steps to Cook

1. Take an Instant Pot; open the top lid.
2. Press "SAUTÉ" cooking function.
3. In the cooking pot area, add the oil and onions.
4. Add the ground beef, salt, turmeric, cilantro, and paprika.
5. Stir the mixture well and sauté it for 4 minutes.
6. Remove the mixture from the pot and set aside.
7. In the pot, add the soy sauce, tomato sauce, and chives. Sauté the mixture for 3 minutes.
8. Add the pasta and chicken stock. Mix in the beef mixture.
9. Close the top lid and make sure the valve is sealed.
10. Press "MANUAL" cooking function. Adjust cooking time to 8 minutes.
11. Allow pressure to build and cook the ingredients for the set time.
12. After the set cooking time ends, press "CANCEL" and then press "QPR". Instant Pot will quickly release pressure.
13. Open the top lid, add the cooked mixture in serving plates.
14. Serve warm.

Servings: 4

SmartPoints: 4

Prep + Cooking Time
30 minutes

Nutritional Values (Per Serving):

- Calories: 183
- Fat: 9g
- Carbohydrates: 1g
- Protein: 24g
- Saturated Fat: 3g
- Sodium: 549mg
- Fiber: 0g

Southern Pork Chops

Ingredients

- 10g sage, chopped
- Salt and pepper
- 680g beef tenderloin
- 10g thyme, chopped
- 2 garlic cloves, sliced
- 10g rosemary, chopped
- 20ml olive oil

Steps to Cook

1. Preheat your oven to 210 degrees C
2. Take a small knife and cut incisions on tenderloin, insert one slice of garlic into the incision
3. Rub meat with oil
4. Take a bowl and add salt, sage, thyme, rosemary, pepper and mix well
5. Rub spice mix over tenderloin
6. Put rubbed tenderloin into roasting pan and bake for 10 minutes
7. Lower temperature to 180 degrees C and cook for 20 minutes more until an internal thermometer read 60 degrees C
8. Transfer tenderloin to cutting board and let them sit for 15 minutes, slice into 20 pieces, and enjoy!

Servings: 4

SmartPoints: 3

Prep + Cooking Time
45 minutes

Nutritional Values (Per Serving):

- Calories: 47
- Fat: 4g
- Carbohydrates: 4g
- Protein: 0.5g
- Saturated Fat: 1g
- Sodium:237mg
- Fiber: 1g

Caramelized Pork Chops And Onion

Ingredients

- 1.8kg chuck roast
- 120g green Chili, chopped
- 30g of chili powder
- 3g of dried oregano
- 3g of cumin, ground
- 2 garlic cloves, minced
- Salt as needed

Steps to Cook

1. Rub the chops with a seasoning of 1 teaspoon of pepper and 2 teaspoons of salt
2. Take a skillet and place it over medium heat, add oil and allow the oil to heat up
3. Brown the seasoned chop both sides
4. Add water and onion to the skillet and cover, lower down the heat to low and simmer for 20 minutes
5. Turn the chops over and season with more salt and pepper
6. Cover and cook until the water fully evaporates and the beer shows a slightly brown texture
7. Remove the chops and serve with a topping of the caramelized onion
8. Serve and enjoy!

Chapter 5:

Vegan And Vegetarian

Vegan And Vegetarian

Servings: 2

SmartPoints: 4

Prep + Cooking Time
40 minutes

Nutritional Values (Per Serving):

- Calories: 400
- Fat: 27g
- Carbohydrates: 23g
- Protein: 26g
- Saturated Fat: 7g
- Sodium: 198mg
- Fiber: 2g

Grilled Sprouts And Balsamic Glaze

Ingredients

- 225g Brussels sprouts, trimmed and halved
- Fresh cracked black pepper
- 15ml olive oil
- Salt to taste
- 10g balsamic glaze
- 2 wooden skewers

Steps to Cook

1. Take wooden skewers and place them on a largely sized foil
2. Place sprouts on the skewers and drizzle oil sprinkle salt and pepper
3. Cover skewers with foil
4. Preheat your grill to low and place skewers (with foil) in the grill
5. Grill for 30 minutes, making sure to turn after every 5-6 minutes
6. Once done, uncovered and drizzle balsamic glaze on top
7. Enjoy!

Vegan And Vegetarian

Servings: 4

SmartPoints: 5

Prep + Cooking Time
10 minutes

Nutritional Values (Per Serving):

- Calories: 395
- Fat: 7g
- Carbohydrates: 42g
- Protein: 35g
- Saturated Fat: 2g
- Sodium: 315mg
- Fiber: 2g

Garbanzo Beans

Ingredients

- 1 can garbanzo beans, chickpeas
- 15ml olive oil
- 5g salt
- 5g garlic powder
- 3g paprika

Steps to Cook

1. Preheat your oven to 190 degrees C
2. Line a baking sheet with silicone baking mat
3. Drain and rinse garbanzo beans, pat garbanzo beans dry and pout into a large bowl
4. Toss with olive oil, salt, garlic powder, paprika and mix well
5. Spread over a baking sheet
6. Bake for 20 minutes at 190 degrees C
7. Turn chickpeas, so they are roasted well
8. Place back in the oven and bake for 25 minutes at 190 degrees C
9. Let them cool and enjoy!

Vegan And Vegetarian

Servings: 6

SmartPoints: 4

Prep + Cooking Time
22 minutes

Nutritional Values (Per Serving):

- Calories - 138
- Fat – 4.5g
- Carbohydrates – 26.5g
- Fiber – 3g
- Sodium - 312mg
- Protein – 5g

Potato Buttermilk Appetizer

Ingredients

- 80ml buttermilk, low-fat
- 3g kosher salt
- 60g sour cream
- 750ml water
- 900g russet potatoes, peeled and make quarters
- 5g salt
- 30g butter
- Parsley as required, chopped
- Black pepper as needed

Steps to Cook

1. Take an Instant Pot; open the top lid.
2. Add the water, salt, and potato in the cooking pot. Using a spatula, gently stir to combine well.
3. Close the top lid and make sure the valve is sealed.
4. Press "MANUAL" cooking function. Adjust cooking time to 10-12 minutes.
5. Allow pressure to build and cook the ingredients for the set time.
6. After the set cooking time ends, press "CANCEL" and then press "QPR". Instant Pot will quickly release pressure.
7. Open the top lid, drain water except for 125g and add the potatoes to a blender. Add 125ml of water also.
8. Add in the remaining ingredients and blend to create a mash like consistency.
9. Serve warm.

Vegan And Vegetarian

Servings: 7-8

SmartPoints: 4

Prep + Cooking Time
30 minutes

Nutritional Values (Per Serving):

- Calories - 112
- Fat – 4.5g
- Carbohydrates – 16g
- Fiber – 3g
- Sodium - 173mg
- Protein – 3g

Orange Glazed Potatoes

Ingredients

- 15g cinnamon
- 15g blackstrap molasses
- 125ml orange juice
- 1kg sweet potatoes make small-sized pieces
- 5g vanilla
- 60g sugar

Steps to Cook

1. In a heat-proof bowl, add the potatoes. Mix in the cinnamon, molasses, sugar, orange juice, and vanilla.
2. Take an Instant Pot; open the top lid.
3. Pour 1 cup water and place steamer basket/trivet inside the cooking pot.
4. Arrange the bowl over the basket/trivet.
5. Close the top lid and make sure the valve is sealed.
6. Press "MANUAL" cooking function. Adjust cooking time to 20-22 minutes.
7. Allow pressure to build and cook the ingredients for the set time.
8. After the set cooking time ends, press "CANCEL" and then press "NPR". Instant Pot will slowly and naturally release the pressure for 8- 10 minutes.
9. Open the top lid, add the cooked mixture in serving plates.
10. Serve warm.

Vegan And Vegetarian

Servings: 4-5

SmartPoints: 1

Prep + Cooking Time
15 minutes

Nutritional Values (Per Serving):

- Calories - 93
- Fat – 5.5g
- Carbohydrates – 4g
- Fiber – 1g
- Sodium - 33mg
- Protein – 4.5g

Broccoli Spinach Greens

Ingredients

- 500g kale, chopped
- 3g cumin, ground
- 500g broccoli, chopped
- 500g baby spinach
- 3g coriander, ground
- 2 cloves garlic, crushed or minced
- 30ml coconut oil
- 15g ginger, minced

Steps to Cook

1. Take an Instant Pot; open the top lid.
2. Press "SAUTÉ" cooking function.
3. In the cooking pot area, add the oil, garlic, ginger, and broccoli. Cook until turn translucent and softened for 4-5 minutes.
4. Add the remaining ingredients.
5. Cook until spinach and kale are wilted.
6. Add the cooked mixture in serving plates.
7. Serve warm.

Servings: 4

SmartPoints: 1

Prep + Cooking Time
20 minutes

Nutritional Values (Per Serving):

- Calories: 368
- Fat: 21g
- Carbohydrates: 34g
- Protein: 1g
- Saturated Fat: 3g
- Sodium: 120mg
- Fiber: 3g

Lovely Apple Slices

Ingredients

- 250ml of coconut oil
- 60g date paste
- 30g ground cinnamon
- 4 granny smith apples, peeled and sliced, cored

Steps to Cook

1. Take a large-sized skillet and place it over medium heat
2. Add oil and allow the oil to heat up
3. Stir in cinnamon and date paste into the oil
4. Add cut up apples and cook for 5-8 minutes until crispy
5. Serve and enjoy!

Vegan And Vegetarian

Servings: 4

SmartPoints: 3

Prep + Cooking Time
35 minutes

Nutritional Values (Per Serving):

- Calories: 270
- Fat: 20g
- Carbohydrates: 10g
- Protein: 15g
- Saturated Fat: 4g
- Sodium: 1235mg
- Fiber: 3g

Amazing Zucchini Boats

Ingredients

- 4 medium zucchinis
- 125ml marinara sauce
- ¼ red onion, sliced
- 60g kalamata olives, chopped
- 125g cherry tomatoes, sliced
- 30g fresh basil

Steps to Cook

1. Preheat your oven to 200 degrees C
2. Cut the zucchini half-lengthwise and shape them in boats
3. Take a bowl and add tomato sauce, spread 1 layer of sauce on top of each of the boat
4. Top with onion, olives, and tomatoes
5. Bake for 20-25 minutes
6. Top with basil and enjoy!

Chapter 6:

Fish And Seafood Recipes

Fish And Seafood Recipes

Servings: 4

SmartPoints: 5

Prep + Cooking Time
10 minutes

Nutritional Values (Per Serving):

- Calories: 246
- Fat: 10g
- Carbohydrates: 14g
- Protein: 27g
- Saturated Fat: 3g
- Sodium: 433mg
- Fiber: 2g

Lobster Salad

Ingredients

- 220g lobster, cooked and chopped
- 850g asparagus, chopped and steamed
- 30ml lemon juice
- 20ml extra virgin olive oil
- 1g kosher salt
- Pepper
- 125g cherry tomatoes halved
- 1 basil leaf, chopped
- 30g red onion, diced

Steps to Cook

1. Whisk in lemon juice, salt, pepper in a bowl and mix with oil
2. Take a bowl and add rest of the ingredients
3. Toss well and pour dressing on top
4. Serve and enjoy!

Fish And Seafood Recipes

Servings: 5

SmartPoints: 6

Prep + Cooking Time
35 minutes

Nutritional Values (Per Serving):

- Calories: 181
- Fat: 7g
- Carbohydrates: 9g
- Protein: 21g
- Saturated Fat: 2g
- Sodium: 327mg
- Fiber: 3g

Spinach And Feta Stuffed Tilapia

Ingredients

- 160g tilapia fillets
- Pinch of salt and pepper
- 1 egg beaten
- 125g part-skim ricotta cheese
- 125g crumbled feta cheese
- 125g breadcrumbs
- 250g fresh spinach leaves, chopped
- 1g salt
- 1g pepper
- 1g dried thyme leaves
- 1 large lemon

Steps to Cook

1. Preheat your oven to 180 degrees C
2. Splash 2-quart heating dish with cooking shower, pat fish dry with paper towels and sprinkle salt and pepper
3. Take a bowl and blend in eggs and ricotta, until smooth
4. Add in feta, bread pieces, spinach, 1g salt, 1g dark pepper, thyme
5. Partition mixture between the fillet and carefully roll the fish, secure using a toothpick
6. Transfer to the heating dish (crease side down) and crush lemon juice on top
7. Cover and cook for 25 minutes, the stuffing should be ready
8. Enjoy!

Fish And Seafood Recipes

Servings: 4

SmartPoints: 1

Prep + Cooking Time
20 minutes

Nutritional Values (Per Serving):

- Calories - 276
- Fat – 12.5g
- Carbohydrates – 6.5g
- Fiber – 2g
- Sodium - 83mg
- Protein – 36.5g

Basil Herbed Salmon

Ingredients

- 1g rosemary
- 3g dried basil
- 2 tomatoes, chopped
- 1g oregano
- 680g wild salmon
- 1g pepper flakes
- 30g balsamic vinegar
- 60g basil, chopped
- Pepper and salt as per taste
- 10ml olive oil
- 250ml water

Steps to Cook

1. Mix the oregano, basil, pepper flakes, pepper, salt and rosemary in a mixing bowl.

2. Use the mix to season the salmon. Wrap and seal the salmon in a baking sheet.

3. Take an Instant Pot; open the top lid.

4. Pour the water and place steamer basket/trivet inside the cooking pot.

5. Arrange the wrapped salmon over the basket/trivet.

6. Close the top lid and make sure the valve is sealed.

7. Press "MANUAL" cooking function. Adjust cooking time to 8-10 minutes.

8. Allow pressure to build and cook the ingredients for the set time.

9. After the set cooking time ends, press "CANCEL" and then press "QPR". Instant Pot will quickly release pressure.

10. Open the top lid, add the cooked mixture in serving plates.

11. Mix the basil, vinegar, tomatoes, pepper, salt, and olive oil in a bowl. Set aside.

12. Serve warm with the tomato mix.

Fish And Seafood Recipes

Servings: 3-4

SmartPoints: 5

Prep + Cooking Time
18 minutes

Nutritional Values (Per Serving):

- Calories - 327
- Fat – 24.5g
- Carbohydrates – 4.5g
- Fiber – 1g
- Sodium - 136mg
- Protein – 28g

Rosemary Buttery Fish Meal

Ingredients

- 60g butter
- 5g sea salt
- 1 red chili pepper, seeded and sliced
- 280g anchovies
- 3g paprika
- 5g dried dill
- 5g rosemary
- 5g red chili flakes
- 15g basil
- 80g breadcrumbs

Steps to Cook

1. Mix the chili flakes, paprika, sea salt, basil, dry dill, and rosemary together in a bowl.
2. Coat the anchovies with the spice mix.
3. Mix in the chili pepper and let the mixture rest for 10 minutes.
4. Take an Instant Pot; open the top lid.
5. Press "SAUTÉ" cooking function.
6. In the cooking pot area, melt the butter.
7. Dip the spiced anchovies in the breadcrumbs and put in the pot.
8. Cook the anchovies for 4 minutes on each side.
9. Drain on paper towel and serve warm.

Servings: 4

SmartPoints: 2

Prep + Cooking Time
20 minutes

Vegetable Salmon Delight

Nutritional Values (Per Serving):

- Calories - 207
- Fat – 6.5g
- Carbohydrates – 8g
- Fiber – 1g
- Sodium - 183mg
- Protein – 23g

Ingredients

- 450g salmon fillet, skin on
- 1 carrot, julienned
- 1 bell pepper, julienned
- 1 zucchini, julienned
- 1/2 lemon, make slices
- 10ml olive oil
- 17g black pepper
- 180ml water
- 1g salt

Steps to Cook

1. Coat the salmon with the oil and season with pepper and salt.
2. Take an Instant Pot; open the top lid.
3. Pour the water and place steamer basket/trivet inside the cooking pot.
4. Arrange the salmon over the basket/trivet.
5. Close the top lid and make sure the valve is sealed.
6. Press "MANUAL" cooking function. Adjust cooking time to 3 minutes.
7. Allow pressure to build and cook the ingredients for the set time.
8. After the set cooking time ends, press "CANCEL" and then press "QPR". Instant Pot will quickly release pressure.
9. Open the top lid, take out the steamer rack and set aside the cooked salmon.
10. Press "SAUTÉ" cooking function.
11. In the cooking pot area, add the oil and vegetables. Cook until turn softened for 2 minutes.
12. Serve the salmon with sautéed vegetables

Fish And Seafood Recipes

Servings: 3

SmartPoints: 5

Prep + Cooking Time
17 minutes

Nutritional Values (Per Serving):

- Calories – 153
- Fat – 6.5g
- Carbohydrates – 8g
- Fiber – 2.5g
- Sodium - 413mg
- Protein – 16g

Wine Marinates Shrimps

Ingredients

- 15ml lemon juice
- 3g lemon zest
- 30g cilantro/CORIANDER
- 30ml apple cider vinegar
- 7g salt
- 3g ground ginger
- 15ml olive oil
- 60ml white wine
- 5g brown sugar
- 7g minced garlic
- 5g nutmeg
- 250ml water
- 2.49kg peeled shrimps, deveined
- 250g parsley

Steps to Cook

1. Chop the cilantro and parsley. Mix the lemon juice, vinegar, lemon zest, salt, white wine, and sugar together in a mixing bowl.

2. Stir the mixture until sugar and salt dissolve completely.

3. Mix the shrimps in the lemon juice mixture. Add the cilantro and parsley and stir well.

4. Mix in the ginger, olive oil, nutmeg, and water. Allow marinating for 15 minutes.

5. Take an Instant Pot; open the top lid.

6. Add the shrimp mix in the cooking pot. Using a spatula, gently stir to combine well.

7. Close the top lid and make sure the valve is sealed.

8. Press "MANUAL" cooking function. Adjust cooking time to 8 minutes.

9. Allow pressure to build and cook the ingredients for the set time.

10. After the set cooking time ends, press "CANCEL" and then press "QPR". Instant Pot will quickly release pressure.

11. Open the top lid, add the cooked mixture in serving plates.

12. Serve warm.

Servings: 4

SmartPoints: 1

Prep + Cooking Time
35 minutes

Bean Shrimp Rice Meal

Nutritional Values (Per Serving):

- Calories - 276
- Fat – 11.5g
- Carbohydrates – 31g
- Fiber – 4g
- Sodium - 623mg
- Protein – 32.5g

Ingredients

- 375g low sodium vegetable broth
- 30g minced garlic
- 250g rice
- 60g butter
- 450g cooked shrimp
- 1 can black beans, rinsed and drained
- Dried cilantro as required

Steps to Cook

1. Take an Instant Pot; open the top lid.
2. Press "SAUTÉ" cooking function.
3. In the cooking pot area, add the butter and rice.
4. Cook for about 2-3 minutes or until it gets a brown texture.
5. Mix in the pepper, garlic, and salt and stir cook for further 2 minutes.
6. Mix in the shrimps, black beans, and broth.
7. Close the top lid and make sure the valve is sealed.
8. Press "MANUAL" cooking function. Adjust cooking time to 4-5 minutes.
9. Allow pressure to build and cook the ingredients for the set time.
10. After the set cooking time ends, press "CANCEL" and thenpress "NPR". Instant Pot will slowly and naturally release the pressure for 8-10 minutes.
11. Open the top lid, add the cooked mixture in serving plates.
12. Serve warm with cilantro on top.

Fish And Seafood Recipes

Servings: 2

SmartPoints: 2

Prep + Cooking Time
15 minutes

Nutritional Values (Per Serving):

- Calories: 125
- Fat: 2g
- Carbohydrates: 6g
- Protein: 21g
- Saturated Fat: 0.4g
- Sodium: 289mg
- Fiber: 1g

Classic Dijon Fish

Ingredients

- 1 perch, flounder or sole fish florets
- 15g Dijon mustard
- 7ml lemon juice
- 5ml low sodium Worcestershire sauce
- 30g Italian seasoned breadcrumbs
- 1 butter-flavored cooking spray

Steps to Cook

1. Preheat your oven to 230 degrees C
2. Take an 11 x 7-inch baking dish and arrange your fillets carefully
3. Take a small-sized bowl and add lemon juice, Worcestershire sauce, mustard and mix it well
4. Pour the mix over your fillet
5. Sprinkle a good amount of breadcrumbs
6. Bake for 12 minutes until fish flakes off easily
7. Cut the fillet in half portions and enjoy!

Fish And Seafood Recipes

Servings: 2

SmartPoints: 0

Prep + Cooking Time
30 minutes

Nutritional Values (Per Serving):

- Calories: 329
- Fat: 23g
- Carbohydrates: 2g
- Protein: 41g
- Saturated Fat: 6g
- Sodium: 978mg
- Fiber: 0.4g

Baked Zucchini Wrapped Fish

Ingredients

- 680G cod fillets, skin removed
- 15g of blackening spices
- 2 zucchinis, sliced lengthwise from to form ribbon
- 7ml of olive oil

Steps to Cook

1. Season the fish fillets with blackening spice
2. Wrap each fish fillets with zucchini ribbons
3. Place fish on a plate
4. Take a skillet and place it over medium heat
5. Pour oil and allow the oil to heat up
6. Add wrapped fish to the skillet and cook each side for 4 minutes
7. Serve and enjoy!

My Top 10 Recipes

Servings:

SmartPoints:

Prep + Cooking Time

Nutritional Values (Per Serving):

Ingredients

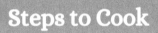

Steps to Cook

Servings:

SmartPoints:

Prep + Cooking Time

Nutritional Values (Per Serving):

Ingredients

Steps to Cook

Servings:

SmartPoints:

Prep + Cooking Time

Nutritional Values (Per Serving):

Ingredients

Steps to Cook

Servings:

SmartPoints:

Prep + Cooking Time

Nutritional Values (Per Serving):

Ingredients

Steps to Cook

Servings:

 SmartPoints:

 **Prep + Cooking Time**

Nutritional Values (Per Serving):

Ingredients

Steps to Cook

Servings:

SmartPoints:

Prep + Cooking Time

Nutritional Values (Per Serving):

Ingredients

Steps to Cook

Servings:

SmartPoints:

Prep + Cooking Time

Nutritional Values (Per Serving):

Ingredients

Steps to Cook

Top 10 Recipes

Servings:

SmartPoints:

Prep + Cooking Time

Nutritional Values (Per Serving):

Ingredients

Steps to Cook

Servings:

SmartPoints:

Prep + Cooking Time

Nutritional Values (Per Serving):

Ingredients

Steps to Cook

Servings:

SmartPoints:

Prep + Cooking Time

Nutritional Values (Per Serving):

Ingredients

Steps to Cook

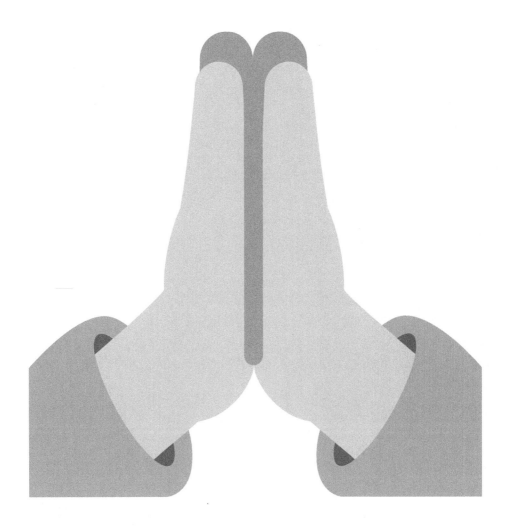

Printed in Great Britain
by Amazon

75073833R00045